# WORKING TOWARD ACHIEVING CIVIL RIGHTS

Tim Cooke

CRABTREE
PUBLISHING COMPANY
WWW.CRABTREEBOOKS.COM

CRABTREE
PUBLISHING COMPANY
WWW.CRABTREEBOOKS.COM

**Author:** Tim Cooke
**Picture Manager:** Sophie Mortimer
**Designer:** Lynne Lennon
**Design Manager:** Keith Davis
**Children's Publisher:** Anne O'Daly
**Editorial director:** Kathy Middleton
**Editor:** Janine Deschenes
**Proofreader:** Wendy Scavuzzo
**Print coordinator:** Katherine Berti



**Photographs:** (t=top, b= bottom, l=left, r=right, c=center)

Front Cover: Alamy: Steven Scott Taylor (center right); Shutterstock: John Gomez (bottom left), Twocoms (bottom center); Wikimedia Commons: Library of Congress (center left)

Interior: Alamy: B Christpher 32, Everett Collection Inc, 34, GL Archive 8, Granger Historical Picture Archive 17, Mark Spowart 36, World History Archive 31; Library of Congress: 14, 19t, 23t; NARA: Roland Scherman 21; Public Domain: Amnesty International/Karen Veldkamp 43, Kambiz Foroohar 37bl, gandhiserve 12, Joe Levine 22, Chris McAndrew 27, Panoramio 28, Godrey Reubens 30, State Library of New South Wales 29b, The Visibility Project Claudette Colvin 18, Yann 13; Shutterstock: Alexander 19b, bacdc 35, bybalet 24, Kobby Dagan 5b, Kojoku 7, Diego G Diaz 38, Everett Collection 9, 11, grejak 4, Jack R Perry Photography 8, Java Designs 41, A Katz 1, 40, Kojoku 7, Lee Snider Photo Images 15, David Mbiyu 25, meunierd 29t, Alexandros michalidis 39, Bill Orchard 26, Snap Sawesdee 23b, stock 37r, Zoltan Tarlacz 10, Rachel Warriner 5t; United Nations: courtesy photo 16; U.S. Government: Florida State and Library Archive 20; Wikimedia Commons: Taylordw 33.

Brown Bear Books has made every attempt to contact the copyright holder. If you have any information about omissions, please contact licensing@brownbearbooks.co.uk

---

Library and Archives Canada Cataloging in Publication

Title: Working toward achieving civil rights / Tim Cooke.
Names: Cooke, Tim, 1961- author.
Description: Series statement: Achieving social change | Includes bibliographical references and index.
Identifiers: Canadiana (print) 20200300407 | Canadiana (print) 20200300415 | Canadiana (ebook) 20200300415 | ISBN 9780778779438 (hardcover) | ISBN 9780778779490 (softcover) | ISBN 9781427125477 (HTML)
Subjects: LCSH: Civil rights—Juvenile literature. | LCSH: Human rights—Juvenile literature.
Classification: LCC JC571 .C66 2021 | DDC j323—dc23

Library of Congress Cataloging-in-Publication Data

Names: Cooke, Tim, 1961- author.
Title: Working toward achieving civil rights / Tim Cooke.
Description: New York : Crabtree Publishing Company, 2021. | Series: Achieving social change | Includes bibliographical references and index.
Identifiers: LCCN 2020032440 (print) | LCCN 2020032441 (ebook) | ISBN 9780778779438 (hardcover) | ISBN 9780778779490 (paperback) | ISBN 9781427125477 (ebook)
Subjects: LCSH: Civil rights--Juvenile literature. | Human rights--Juvenile literature.
Classification: LCC JC571 .C667 2021 (print) | LCC JC571 (ebook) | DDC 323--dc23
LC record available at https://lccn.loc.gov/2020032440
LC ebook record available at https://lccn.loc.gov/2020032441

---

Crabtree Publishing Company
www.crabtreebooks.com 1-800-387-7650

**Published in Canada**
**Crabtree Publishing**
616 Welland Ave.
St. Catharines, ON
L2M 5V6

**Published in the United States**
**Crabtree Publishing**
347 Fifth Ave
Suite 1402-145
New York, NY 10016

Published by CRABTREE PUBLISHING COMPANY in 2021



Printed in the U.S.A./092020/CG20200810

# CONTENTS

# INTRODUCTION

**Civil rights are rights that belong to all citizens of a particular country. They are usually related to ensuring that everyone is treated fairly and has the same opportunities.**

Civil rights are often protected by **constitutions** or laws. For much of history, however, some people have been excluded from the rights given to other citizens. Groups have been segregated, or separated, from the rest of the population on the basis of race. They have been given inferior services such as education and housing, and denied equal opportunities for success. LGBTQ+ people have been denied the right to marry. People in wheelchairs have been physically unable to enter state buildings lacking facilities such as ramps.

*Disability **activists** advocate for policies and solutions that give people with disabilities equal opportunities.*

*Americans protest a decision by the government to define **gender** as being unchangeable. They say this infringes on the rights of **transgender** people.*

## Changing Situation

Activists have tried to improve civil rights for more than a century. The best-known civil rights struggle was in the 1950s and 1960s when Black Americans fought to end racial **discrimination** in American laws, but there have been many others. Activists campaigned to gain legal **status**, equal opportunities, and greater **sovereignty** for **Indigenous** peoples, for example, or for LGBTQ+ people to have the same rights as straight people.

Some civil rights campaigns have continued for decades. Others, such as campaigns for migrants or transgender people, are more recent. Because civil rights are granted by governments, they can change. This means civil rights activism protects and extends rights already gained, as well as taking up the struggle for new rights.

*In 2020, just 30 countries in the world allowed gay couples to marry, which activists argue is a basic civil right.*

CHAPTER 1

# WHAT ARE CIVIL RIGHTS?

**Simply by being born, people are entitled to rights, such as the right to live and not to be subjected to torture. Such rights are universal. They apply to everyone, everywhere. These rights are usually called human rights.**

Civil liberties are similar to human rights. They are freedoms to which everyone in a country is entitled, such as free speech and privacy. Civil rights, however, are similar to civil liberties, but they are not universal. Governments only grant them to specific groups.

Civil rights are concerned with the treatment of individuals. They protect people from discrimination based on race, gender, religion, age, disability, or sexuality. It is a violation of a worker's civil rights, for example, to deny them a promotion based solely on their race or whether they are male or female.

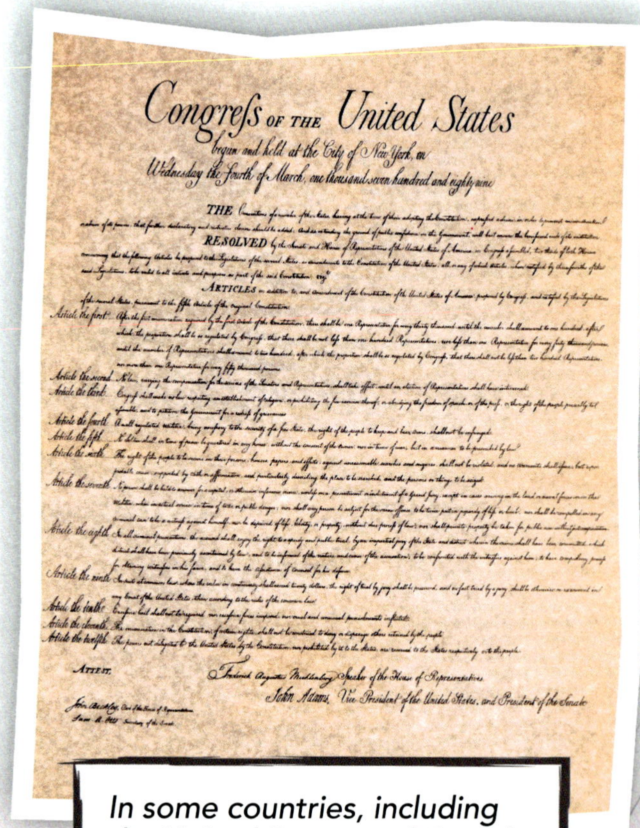
Congress of the United States
begun and held at the City of New-York, on
Wednesday the fourth of March, one thousand seven hundred and eighty nine

*In some countries, including the United States and Canada, rights are written down in what are called bills of rights.*

*Musician Nadya Tolokonnikova is arrested at a Gay Pride march in favor of LGBTQ+ rights in Russia in 2011. Civil rights protestors are often arrested in Russia.*

## Changing Attitudes

Civil rights often reflect the values of society as a whole. Russia is socially **conservative**, and LGBTQ+ people there do not have the same rights as other people. They are not protected from discrimination in employment, for example, and same-sex marriages are forbidden. Civil rights activism often concentrates on changing a particular society's ideas and attitudes.

The American civil rights movement of the 1950s and 1960s was based mainly in Black American churches and colleges. It involved marches, **boycotts**, and **civil disobedience**, such as **sit-ins**, to publicize the complaints of the protestors. The American civil rights movement inspired others, including the civil rights movement in Northern Ireland, disability activism, and LGBTQ+ campaigns.

# Early Ideas About Rights

**The term civil rights comes from the Latin *ius civis*, or "the rights of a citizen." Ancient Greek and Roman citizens, who were all male, had rights that non-citizens, such as women or enslaved people, did not.**

In ancient times, rulers around the world gave certain rights to citizens, who were usually adult males. Such rights included the right to own private property or to worship freely. In return, citizens were expected to acknowledge the authority of the ruler.

By the **Middle Ages**, ties between rulers and their subjects were complex. In 1215, however, **nobles** in England forced King John I to grant some rights to his subjects in the Magna Carta, or "great **charter**." The charter limited the powers of the king. It protected citizens from unjust imprisonment, and gave them the right to a full trial.

*King John only signed Magna Carta because he was an unpopular ruler who needed the support of his nobles.*

*American Patriots fought the Revolution on the grounds that the British government denied their basic rights.*

## The Americas

As they conquered much of the world during the so-called Age of Discovery, Europeans began to consider what rights to give to Indigenous peoples—and also people at home. Spaniards in the Caribbean agreed on a set of rights for Indigenous peoples in 1512, although those rights were often ignored in reality. Indigenous peoples were forced into enslavement to labor for the Spanish, for example.

In 1689, the English Parliament passed the Bill of Rights. Based on the idea of natural rights that were given to humans by God, it protected citizens from, among other things, "cruel and unusual punishment." The English law applied in North America, but some Americans called for a greater say in deciding their own future. They complained that their English rulers raised their taxes from them but gave them no say in how those taxes were spent. Such complaints eventually led to the American Revolution (1775–1783). In 1776, Americans declared independence as the United States of America. At the end of the revolution, American politicians drew up rights for their own citizens.

# Viewpoints

**In July 1789, French revolutionaries, or rebels, rose up against their rulers. They replaced the king with a government of citizens. In August, the new government issued the *Declaration of the Rights of Man and of the Citizen.***

The French document was inspired by England's Magna Carta and the U.S. Declaration of Independence of 1776. That document had claimed that all men "had been created equal" and had also been given "**unalienable**" rights by God. Those rights included "Life, Liberty, and the Pursuit of Happiness." In the French version, the similar phrase was "Men are born and remain free and equal in rights."

*The slogan of the French Revolution—"Liberty, Equality, Brotherhood"—did not apply to women in France or, for example, Black people in French **colonies**.*

The U.S. Constitution was adopted in 1787, followed in 1791 by the Bill of Rights. The bill included 10 **amendments** to the Constitution that limited the power of the government by granting rights to individual citizens.

## Extending Rights to All

In France and the United States, it was clear that the documents gave rights to all groups in society. In France, Olympe de Gouges wrote her own *Declaration of the Rights of Woman and of the Female*, as women were excluded from the original. In the United States, rights were not extended to Native Americans or to enslaved Africans. The history of civil rights activism is, in some ways, the story of fighting to make governments extend rights to everyone.

CHAPTER 2

# THE EMERGENCE OF CIVIL RIGHTS

**In his jail cell in India, Mohandas Gandhi refused to eat. It was 1932, and India's British rulers had introduced a new voting system. Gandhi feared it would reduce the rights of India's lowest** caste**—the Untouchables.**

Gandhi went for six days without food before the British backed down. This was one of 17 hunger strikes he undertook in a lifetime of activism. The longest lasted 29 days. As a leader of Indian politics, Gandhi used fasting, or going without food or drink, as a high-profile way to achieve his goal of Indian independence from British rule. He was jailed 11 times. Soon after achieving his goal, in 1948, he was **assassinated**.

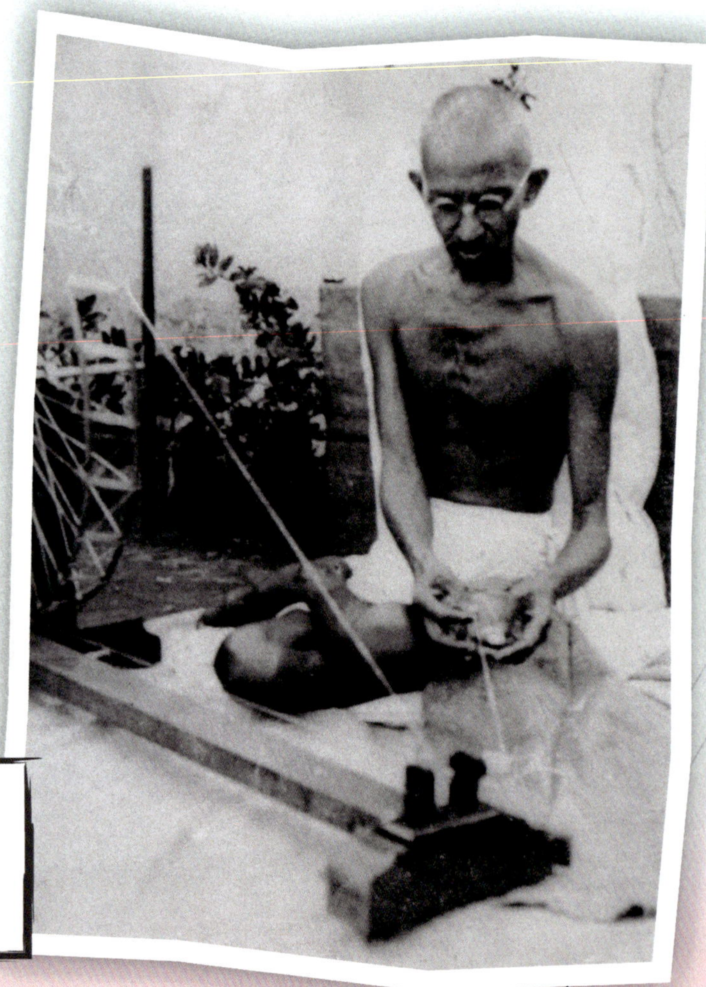

*Gandhi took up traditional spinning to encourage Indians to make their own cloth rather than buy British textiles.*

## Setting an Example

Gandhi was one of the most famous civil rights campaigners of the first half of the 1900s. His ideas of peaceful protest and **non-cooperation** set an example for other activists later in the century, such as Martin Luther King, Jr., who led the civil rights movement in the United States. Fasts, strikes, sit-ins, and marches became established as peaceful ways for campaigners to set out to achieve civil rights.

> This is a god-given opportunity to offer my life as a final service to the downtrodden.
>
> Mohandas K. Gandhi

*Gandhi led a 240-mile (386 km) march to gather salt at the coast. At the time, only the British were allowed to collect salt, so the march was a direct challenge to their rule.*

# Rights for the Excluded

**People most likely to be denied civil rights in most societies were women, ethnic minorities, and Indigenous peoples.**

Women won the right to vote in the 1920s. In many countries, however, women were not protected from discrimination at work until the end of the 20th century. The campaign to gain rights was led by groups such as the National Organization for Women (NOW), founded in 1966.

In 1909, activists set up the National Association for the Advancement of Colored People (NAACP). It brought legal cases to challenge Jim Crow laws that were introduced after the abolition of slavery. Those laws segregated the races in the South and prevented Black Americans from voting.

*W.E.B. Du Bois was the only Black American on the original board of the NAACP, and founded its journal* The Crisis, *which is still published.*

## Key Events

### Power in Numbers

Indigenous peoples in North America worked together to fight for civil rights, such as sovereignty over their lands. The National Congress of American Indians (NCAI) was founded in 1944. It was the first nationwide organization to campaign for Indigenous civil rights in the United States. In Canada, the National Indian Council (now the Assembly of First Nations) was founded in 1961 for similar purposes.

The NAACP still exists today. The American Civil Liberties Union (ACLU) also survives after a century of protecting civil rights. It was formed in 1920 by lawyers worried about civil liberties after World War I. The Canadian Civil Liberties Association (CCLA) was founded in 1964 to fight for changes to the laws to improve rights. Each year, ACLU and CCLA attorneys represent thousands of people from all backgrounds whose rights have been violated.

## Working Together

Organizations have proved to be extremely important in fighting for the civil rights of all people. The first organization to represent disabled Americans, the National Association for the Deaf, was founded in 1880. Until nearly a century later, however, there was little concerted attempt to establish rights for disabled people.

*ACLU supporters march in a Gay Pride event in New York City. The ACLU leads the legal fight for civil rights in America.*

# Growing Recognition

**In the aftermath of World War II (1939–1945), Gandhi's protests in India and the suffering left by the conflict led to a wider acceptance that basic rights should apply to every individual.**

One result was the Universal Declaration of Human Rights (UDHR), adopted in 1948 by the United Nations. The UDHR included human rights, such as the right to life. It included **economic** rights, such as the right to safety in the workplace; and it included rights granted by governments, such as the right to vote. The UDHR provided a model for later rights legislation, including Canada's Bill of Rights in 1960 and Charter of Rights and Freedoms in 1982, and the UK Human Rights Act of 1998.

*Eleanor Roosevelt studies an early copy of the UDHR. It is said to be the most translated document in the world.*

*Black students face an unfriendly welcome at a **desegregated** school. It was a brave choice for families to stand up for their right to an equal education with White children.*

## Ending Segregation

The wartime service of Black Americans and other minorities was changing perceptions of civil rights in the United States. In 1954, NAACP lawyers challenged the "separate but equal" legal idea by which Black children could be educated separately from White children. They argued that provisions for Black children were inferior to those made for White children. The U.S. Supreme Court decision in *Brown v. Board of Education* made segregation in education illegal, or not allowed by law. When the high school at Little Rock in Arkansas refused to integrate in 1957, the government sent federal troops to enforce desegregation.

## Key Voices

### First Lady of Human Rights

As First Lady from 1933 to 1945, Eleanor Roosevelt was a high-profile supporter of the campaign for Black rights. After World War II, she became the first American delegate to the UN General Assembly, and chairwoman of the UN Commission on Human Rights. She played a leading role in writing the UDHR and having it **ratified**.

CHAPTER 3

# NORTH AMERICAN CIVIL RIGHTS

**Claudette Colvin was tired after school in Montgomery, Alabama, and the bus was full. When a White woman got on and there was no room in the White section, the driver asked Claudette and the woman next to her to give up their seats in the colored section.**

Claudette and the woman refused. It was Negro History Week in March 1955, and Claudette had been studying civil rights. She later said, "My head was just too full of black history." Police removed Colvin from the bus, and she spent the night in prison. In Canada, Viola Desmond had made a similar protest in 1946. She refused to move from the Whites-only section of a theater in New Glasgow, Nova Scotia. Viola's resistance inspired the Canadian civil rights movement.

*Fifteen-year-old Claudette Colvin protested that she had a constitutional right to remain in her seat on the bus.*

> "It felt like Sojourner Truth was on one side pushing me down and Harriet Tubman was on the other side pushing me down."
>
> Claudette Colvin, on staying in her seat

*The interstate transportation system was segregated, with separate facilities and areas for Black customers and White customers.*

## Bus Boycott in Montgomery

Nine months after Claudette Colvin's protest, a Black seamstress named Rosa Parks also refused to give up her seat on a bus in Montgomery. Parks became the figurehead of a boycott that eventually forced the city to desegregate public transportation. The boycott was organized by the Southern Christian Leadership Conference. A leading role in the protest was taken by a young preacher named Martin Luther King, Jr.

# Nonviolent Resistance

**The civil rights movement of the 1950s and 1960s led to a series of laws such as the Civil Rights Act of 1964. The movement was inspired by the nonviolent protests of Gandhi.**

In February 1960, four Black students refused to leave a segregated lunch counter in Woolworths in Greensboro, North Carolina. They were joined by hundreds more protestors. Woolworths was forced to desegregate their lunch counters. Other sit-ins followed, coordinated by the Student Nonviolent Coordinating Committee, an interracial group that used nonviolent tactics to fight for civil rights.

In 1961, 13 students—seven Black and six White—set off on a Freedom Ride through Alabama, Mississippi, and North Carolina to protest segregated bus terminals. This led to the government desegregating bus terminals.

*Activist Benjamin Cowins waits for service during a sit-in at a Whites-only lunch counter in Tallahassee, Florida.*

*Martin Luther King, Jr. was an inspirational speaker. He had learned his skills as a Baptist minister preaching to his congregation.*

## Facing Down Violence

The movement also used marches to gain publicity. On August 28, 1963, more than 250,000 people marched in Washington, DC, to urge the government to adopt civil rights legislation, which it did the following July. In 1965, a march in Alabama from Selma to Montgomery calling for voting rights ended in police beating and gassing the marchers. Throughout the civil rights struggle, activists faced beatings, abuse, and arrest. In 1968, two prominent civil rights leaders Malcolm X and Dr. Martin Luther King, Jr. were assassinated but the movement remained largely true to the idea of nonviolence. It eventually overturned all the Jim Crow laws that supported legal segregation. Black Americans still faced discrimination, however, and peaceful protest continues to claim better civil rights for them.

## Key Voices

### Black Power

The Black Power movement called for more aggressive resistance to the brutality faced by Black people. A group named the Black Panthers set up armed patrols in Oakland, California, to resist what they saw as police brutality toward Black Americans. They also created social programs to support Black communities and businesses.

# Other Movements

**Alongside the Black civil rights movement, other groups lobbying for better rights included Mexican Americans and Indigenous peoples in the United States and Canada.**

Mexican American activists founded groups such as the Mexican American Legal Defense and Educational Fund (MALDEF). They wanted more political rights for Mexican Americans. They promoted the idea that **Chicanos**, or Mexican Americans, had a distinct identity. MALDEF, founded in 1968, was modeled on the NAACP. In 1967, students frustrated with the lack of increased rights formed the more **militant** Mexican American Youth Organization (MAYO). It used tactics such as student walkouts to gain control of school boards.

*Union organizer César Chávez (right) improved the conditions of Mexican farm workers in California.*

## Gaining Publicity

A militant approach was shared by the American Indian Movement (AIM). AIM called for rights such as sovereignty over tribal lands. It staged acts of civil disobedience such as the **occupation** of Wounded Knee in 1973. In Canada, the National Indian Brotherhood (NIB) was formed in 1968, as was the Native Council of Canada. Such organizations gave different peoples a single voice. This made the views of First Nations harder for the government to ignore.

*Activists pitched tipis in Washington, DC, in 1978 after marching across the country in 1978 to persuade the government to honor treaties made with Native Americans.*

## Key Events

### Occupation of Alcatraz

In November 1969, Native Americans landed on Alcatraz Island in San Francisco (right). Calling themselves Indians of All Tribes (IOAT), they claimed the land. The 19-month occupation made many people aware of the issue of land rights for the first time.

CHAPTER 4

# RIGHTS AROUND THE WORLD

**In 2016, Joycelyn John flew from London to Grenada, in the Caribbean. Joycelyn's parents were part of the Windrush Generation. This name was given to Caribbean people who moved to Britain to work after World War II.**

The new arrivals were named after the *Empire Windrush*, a ship that brought the first Caribbean workers to Britain in 1948. The government of the time welcomed them to fill jobs as Britain recovered from the effects of the war. But, it did not give the new arrivals papers that proved they were allowed to live and work in the country. This right was automatic at the time. Then, in the 2000s, the British government targeted immigrants. The Windrush Generation got caught up in this. They were told to prove their right to be in Britain. Many could not, because they did not have papers. Although Joycelyn had lived in Britain for more than 50 years, she was **deported**.

*Joycelyn John lost her job and her home before deciding she had little choice but to agree to move to Grenada.*

*Resistance to the deportations was led by the Windrush Generation themselves. They suggested they were brought to Britain to do "donkey work" the British did not want to do.*

## Campaign Success

Thousands of people lost their jobs and homes, or were sent to countries they had never visited. A journalist began to collect their stories, and campaigners staged protests. Eventually, the government was shamed into backing down. It gave more than 6,000 people the right to live in Britain—including Joycelyn John, who flew back home in July 2018.

> We got angry, did things right, and it's still a journey we have to keep going on with.
>
> Michael Braithwaite
> Windrush campaigner

# No Welcome

**Black and Asian people arriving in Britain in the 1950s and 1960s faced discrimination in housing and in employment. The law at the time did not protect them.**

Some landlords refused to rent out rooms to immigrants, while some employers refused to hire them because of racism. A trade union representing bus workers in Bristol urged the bus company to refuse to employ nonwhite workers. Inspired by the bus boycott in Montgomery, Alabama, Paul Stephenson, Bristol's first Black youth officer, organized a boycott of Bristol buses in 1963. The campaign was supported by thousands of people. After 60 days, the bus company backed down.

*A man reads a sign in a boardinghouse window in the UK in 1964. Many landlords refused to rent rooms to Black and Asian people. Signs like this were common in the 1950s and 1960s.*

## Campaigning Voices

The following year, Martin Luther King, Jr., visited Britain. He was on his way from the United States to Sweden to collect the 1964 Nobel Prize for Peace. King met with Black and White community leaders in London and inspired them to create the Campaign Against Racial Discrimination (CARD). CARD was one of a number of **pressure groups** whose campaigns led to the passage of race relations acts that gradually reduced cases where Black people in Britain were discriminated against in housing and employment. CARD used tactics such as mail-in campaigns for its supporters to put pressure on their members of parliament.

*The lawyer and politician Anthony Lester, later Lord Lester, was one of the founding members of CARD.*

### Key Events

#### Britain's Race Relations Acts

Activists in the United Kingdom eventually forced the government to pass a series of Race Relations acts. The act of 1965 made it illegal to discriminate against anyone in public places on the grounds of race. Campaigners' efforts resulted in a new act in 1968, which forbade discrimination in housing and employment. A further act in 1976 made it illegal to treat someone less favorably due to their race.

# Fighting for Rights

**Around the world, other groups campaigned for civil rights in the 1960s and 1970s. Some were inspired by the civil rights movement in the United States.**

In Northern Ireland, the Northern Ireland Civil Rights Association (NICRA) was set up in 1967 to call for an end to discrimination against the Catholic minority. Catholics found it more difficult to get jobs or access social housing than the Protestant majority. They also lacked equal voting rights in local elections. NICRA began a campaign of civil disobedience to persuade Northern Ireland's British government to improve their rights. However, in 1968, some clashes between activists and the police became increasingly violent.

*A mural in Derry commemorates Bloody Sunday, in January 1972, when British soldiers shot 26 unarmed protestors during a civil rights march, killing 14 people.*

## Key Events

### The Quiet Revolution

In Quebec, Canada, French Canadians wanted more control over their own affairs. In the 1960s, they began a campaign of strikes and marches to take more political control of Quebec from the Canadian government. They also passed laws to protect the French language in organizations such as McGill University (right).

## Australian Freedom Rides

In Australia, Students for **Aboriginal** Action were inspired by the Freedom Rides in the United States to organize a bus tour of Aboriginal communities in New South Wales in 1965. The Australian Freedom Ride revealed the racism often faced by Aboriginal people, and that their rights were often ignored. The students protested outside segregated facilities such as parks, swimming pools, and pubs. In 1967, the government changed the constitution to start to improve the rights of Aboriginal communities.

*Activists interview two Aboriginal women (standing, right) during the Australian Freedom Ride of 1965.*

# South Africa

**In South Africa, the White minority excluded Black Africans from voting in 1948. They also introduced apartheid—a form of segregation that left Black people living in poor conditions in townships and subject to legal controls.**

The struggle to achieve civil rights for Black South Africans was led by the African National Congress (ANC). Among the activists inspired to join the ANC were young lawyers named Nelson Mandela and Oliver Tambo. They organized civil disobedience based on that used by Gandhi in India. When the government refused to shift their position, Mandela created an armed branch of the ANC ready to start a **guerrilla** war against the government.

*This painting shows the incident in 1960, when police killed 69 marchers protesting the introduction of identity papers for Black South Africans.*

*Lawyers Oliver Tambo (left) and Nelson Mandela coordinated a campaign of civil disobedience that eventually led to their arrest.*

## End of a Long Struggle

Before the war could begin, Mandela and 10 other ANC leaders were tried for political offenses and sentenced to life in prison. Other activists continued to fight apartheid, including student groups, churches, and trade unions.

There was also international activism for change. Many sports teams refused to visit South Africa, which was also excluded from the Olympic Games. Individual musicians and actors refused to perform there. Financial companies stopped investing in the country. The pressure forced the South African government to act. In 1990, after 27 years in prison, Mandela was finally released and Black Africans were given voting rights. In 1994, Mandela was elected as the country's first Black president.

### Key Events

#### International Boycott

Individuals in the United Kingdom protested apartheid by refusing to buy South African **exports** starting in 1959. A poll in 1986 suggested that 27 percent of British people were boycotting South African goods, such as fruit and vegetables. Individuals in other countries also boycotted goods from South Africa.

CHAPTER 5

# RIGHTS FOR ALL

**In spring 1977, 120 protestors took part in the 504 Sit-In, which lasted almost a month. Inside the Federal Building at 50 United Nations Plaza in San Francisco, where the sit-in took place, life was tough. The protestors slept in sleeping bags and ate hot meals delivered by the Black Panther civil rights group.**

The protestors all had physical disabilities, ranging from blindness to **quadriplegia**. Many were without their caregivers, so they had to learn to help one another. The activists were protesting the failure to implement legislation to make it unlawful to discriminate against disabled people in any services that relied on federal funds. For the first time, activists with all types of disabilities joined together as part of nationwide protests.

*ADAPT activists in Washington, DC, in 2017 protest threatened cuts to Medicaid. ADAPT fights for rights to financial support and access to public transportation.*

*Judith Heumann went to court to force the education board to let her become a teacher. She had been refused permission because she used a wheelchair. She later became a special advisor to President Barack Obama on disability rights.*

## Taking the Lead

One leader of the sit-in was Judith E. Heumann. In 1970, Heumann had set up Disabled in Action, which organized sit-ins and other actions. Other activists used similar tactics. In Denver in 1978, 19 activists with disabilities blocked buses to highlight the lack of wheelchair accessibility.

Contemporary activists argue that people are not limited by physical or mental disabilities but by social barriers, such as lack of facilities. In what is termed the "social model of disability," civil rights are essential to ensuring that everyone has the chance to achieve their potential.

Social media has proved valuable in spreading activists' messages. The viral Wouldn't Change a Thing campaign, for example, featured mothers and children who have Down Syndrome using sign language to participate in carpool karaoke. The campaign helps dispel stereotypes about the condition.

"We are beautiful, we are powerful, we are strong, we are important."

504 Sit-In Activist

# Fighting for LGBTQ+ Rights

Homosexuality **was illegal in most countries until the 1960s. LGBTQ+ people lacked rights such as being able to marry their partner or being protected against discrimination.**

In the United States, homosexuality was officially classed as a mental illness until Barbara Gittings, a lesbian activist, held public debates with psychiatrists to persuade them to take homosexuality off the list of mental illnesses in 1972. Meanwhile, gay protestors marched every July 4 from 1965 to 1969 to highlight their inability even to gather with other LGBTQ+ people. The situation changed in 1969, after New York police raided the Stonewall Inn, a gay bar in Greenwich Village. They had targeted the bar before, but this time, clients resisted. Two nights of rioting broke out. The Stonewall Riots marked the beginning of a new form of LGBTQ+ rights campaigning. Gay activism had evolved from low-key protests to embracing one's sexuality with the slogan "gay pride."

*Drag queen Marsha P. Johnson was an LGBTQ+ activist and one of the key people who stood up to the police when they raided the Stonewall Inn.*

*Activists protest to protect LGBTQ+ people against discrimination at work outside the U.S. Supreme Court in 2019. The court outlawed such discrimination the following year.*

## Pride in Canada

In Canada, LGBTQ+ activism also became more visible. In February 1981, police raided gay **bathhouses** in Toronto, arresting many people. The next day, 3,000 people marched to protest the raids. Meanwhile, provincial laws began to extend equal protection under the law to all Canadians, regardless of sexual orientation.

## Key Events

### Pride Parades

The first Gay Pride marches were held in 1970 in New York, Chicago, and Los Angeles as a reaction to the Stonewall Riots. Pride marches now happen all over the world. Toronto's first parade took place in 1981, after police raids in the city. In 1991, it was endorsed as an official event by the city authorities.

CHAPTER 6

# CIVIL RIGHTS TODAY

**The fight for civil rights continues. In different countries around the world, Black, Indigenous, LGBTQ+, and activists with disabilities are seeking to protect or extend their civil rights.**

In 2012, for example, three First Nations women in Canada founded Idle No More. The movement campaigns for First Nations to maintain sovereignty over their own affairs and to prevent the exploitation of resources on First Nations land. They organize peaceful protests such as railroad blockades and flash-mob **round dances** to gain publicity. As a result, First Nations chiefs were invited to meet government and opposition politicians to ensure their rights to institute environmental policies on their own lands.

*Idle No More activists take part in a flash mob in London, Ontario, in 2013. That same year, activists marched 995 miles (1,600 km) from their homes in Quebec to Ottawa.*

In the United States, Black Americans are **incarcerated** in state prisons at more than five times the rate of White Americans. The fight against this injustice is led by the American Civil Liberties Union (ACLU). The ACLU takes court action and pushes for changes to policing and legal policies that discriminate against Black people.

## Worldwide Action

Civil rights are under threat around the world. In Pakistan and Afghanistan, Islamists oppose the education of girls. In China, political opponents of the government are detained without trial, and Uganda wants to introduce the death penalty for homosexuality. One voice resisting such moves is Venezuelan activist Thor Halvorssen, who started the Human Rights Foundation in 2005. He also founded the Oslo Freedom Forum, an annual meeting of some of the world's leading human rights activists.

*Malala Yousafzai was 15 when she was shot and nearly killed by the Taliban terrorist group for promoting girls' education in Pakistan. She is now a leader in the fight for girls' education worldwide.*

### Key Voices

#### Uncovered Journalist

Masih Alinejad campaigns against rules about women's clothing in Iran, where the law makes women wear a headscarf in public. Her Facebook page, My Stealthy Freedom, encourages women to post images of themselves without a headscarf.

# Migrant Rights

**More than eight percent of the world population is made up of migrants fleeing violence or poverty. They often lack civil rights because they are not citizens of the country where they live.**

Activists keep pressure on governments to welcome **refugees**. In 2014, German activists set up Refugees Welcome International, which arranges for refugees to stay in private homes in 16 European countries. The Home Is Here Coalition, meanwhile, was set up to use legal action to protect the Dreamers, migrant children raised in the United States. The government seeks to end a program that allowed them to remain in the United States, threatening to send them "home" to countries that many of them have never even visited. In 2020, the Supreme Court upheld the rights of the Dreamers to remain in the United States.

*There are about 256,000 Dreamers in the United States. Their ability to remain depends on the continuation of legislation known as DACA.*

*Activists in northern Europe campaign to encourage their governments to accept migrants arriving in the European Union.*

## Campaign for a Classmate

Nonso Muojeke's family arrived in Ireland in 2007, when they fled violence in their homeland of Nigeria. In 2018, the family was threatened with deportation as illegal immigrants. Nonso's classmates used an online campaign to gather 22,000 signatures on a petition. Eventually, the government gave in and the family was allowed to stay. A group of schoolchildren had campaigned against the national government—and won.

**Key Voices**

### Speaking up for Refugee Children

Czech-born Lord Alf Dubs was one of hundreds of Jewish children who came to Britain on the Kindertransport to escape the Nazi occupation of Czechoslovakia in 1939. As a politician, Dubs brought forward legislation in 2016 to allow unaccompanied child refugees into Britain. Although the plan was adopted, it was later dropped.

# Black Lives Matter

**Changing civil rights is difficult because unequal treatment of social groups is often coded into law. The Black Lives Matter (BLM) campaign highlights the** systemic racism **faced by Black people in many countries.**

BLM began in 2013 as a hashtag. It was sparked by the acquittal in court of a man who confronted and killed Trayvon Martin, an unarmed Black teen, in Florida. State laws in Florida allowed such confrontations where a person felt threatened. Some accounts highlighted the hoodie Martin wore as making him seem more threatening. BLM supporters claimed that such laws encourage **racial profiling** and thus create situations in which Black Americans and other people of color are treated differently from White Americans.

*Mass marches are a key way for BLM to gather supporters and gain publicity for its cause by starting a public debate.*

*Pressure from BLM activists led to the decision of the Quaker Oats company to rebrand its Aunt Jemima syrup in June 2020. Activists said the Aunt Jemima figure reflected a racist stereotype.*

## Changing Ideas, Changing Government

In 2020, police killed George Floyd in Minneapolis by kneeling on his neck for 8 minutes, 46 seconds. BLM coordinated protests all over the country and around the world. In many places, gatherings were violently broken up by the police and federal officers. In others, the police joined the protests. In some places, protestors pulled down statues of people who supported slavery, such as leaders of the **Confederacy** and those who had profited from slavery.

## Key Events

### Taking the Knee

After the death of George Floyd, BLM activists began protesting by dropping to one knee, often for 8 minutes, 46 seconds. Taking the Knee, which shows both respect and resistance, was also used by Martin Luther King, Jr. in the 1960s. In 2016, it was adopted by activists such as football player Colin Kaepernick, who knelt during the national anthem to protest police treatment of Black Americans.

# GET INVOLVED

**Civil rights reflect the histories, values, and laws of particular societies. Activism often takes the form of raising awareness of groups whose rights are under threat.**

## 1 Be Local

One direct way to become involved is to be aware of possible civil rights issues in your area. If you do become aware of a particular cause, find out if anyone is working to bring it to local attention and offer to help. You could write your political representatives and the press to explain the problem, or you could gather signatures on a petition.

## 2 Volunteer

Local, national, and international rights groups always need volunteers. The ACLU in the United States, the Canadian Civil Liberties Association, or Liberty in the United Kingdom are among groups that rely on volunteers to raise money, run events, hand out leaflets, or help in the office. Use the Internet to research groups near you and decide which causes you feel most strongly about.

## 3 Raise Money

Most civil rights organizations are charities, so they rely on money from the public. You could try raising money for particular organizations through events such as yard sales or sponsored activities with your friends.

## 4 Get Informed

Civil rights activism includes staying up-to-date about changing civil rights issues in your country and around the world. Set up Internet alerts for breaking news about civil rights, or follow activists on social media. Make sure to gather information from many sources and check reliable websites, such as civil rights organizations.

## 5 Show Up!

Civil rights activists often organize marches and other mass events to highlight a particular cause. Watch for events near you, and go along if you can. Large-scale events are great ways to gain publicity, and the more people that attend, the greater the exposure.

# Timeline

**1909** The National Association for the Advancement of Colored People (NAACP) is founded in New York.

**1920** The American Civil Liberties Union (ACLU) is founded.

**1932** In India, Mohandas K. Gandhi holds his first hunger strike.

**1944** The National Congress of American Indians is founded after Native American service in World War II.

**1946** Viola Desmond refuses to leave the White section of a theater in Nova Scotia—a key moment in the civil rights movement in Canada.

**1954** NAACP lawyers persuade the Supreme Court to outlaw segregation in education.

**1956** A year-long public boycott leads to the desegregation of buses in Montgomery, Alabama.

**1963** More than 250,000 people join the March on Washington to claim better rights for Black Americans.

**1963** In Bristol, UK, a boycott forces the bus company to change a policy outlawing Black workers.

**1969** Activists occupy Alcatraz Island in San Francisco to highlight Native American land rights.

**1969** A riot breaks out when police raid the Stonewall Inn in New York City. The event leads to a new type of gay rights activism.

**1972** Aboriginal activists set up a "tent assembly" outside the Australian parliament to protest land rights.

**1977** Disabled activists hold the 504 Sit-In in San Francisco and other cities to protest the slow progress of disability rights legislation.

**1994** Nelson Mandela is elected president in South Africa's first fully democratic elections.

**2012** Canadian activists form Idle No More to fight for First Nations sovereignty and land protection.

**2013** Black Lives Matter (BLM) is formed when the killer of Black American Trayvon Martin is freed by a court.

**2018** The Windrush campaign forces the British government to allow long-term immigrants from the Caribbean to remain in the country.

**2020** BLM coordinates global protests following the police killing of George Floyd in Minneapolis.

# Sources


**Chapter 1**

"The Bill of Rights: A Brief History." American Civil Liberties Union. https://bit.ly/2XBUqbH

"A Brief History of Civil Rights in the United States." Georgetown Law. guides.ll.georgetown.edu/civilrights

Weller, Karina. "Magna Carta: The Origin of Modern Human Rights." Each Other. April 2017. eachother.org.uk/magna-carta-rights-today

**Chapter 2**

"A Brief History of Jim Crow." Constitutional Rights Foundation. https://bit.ly/31tjqmC

Choudhurie, Ramananda. "Gandhian philosophy of Satyagraha." Bombay Sarvodaya Mandal. www.mkgandhi.org/articles/ramanand.htm

Faville, Andrea. "A Civil Rights History: Native Americans." Knight Chair in Political Reporting. 2012. https://bit.ly/33F7v8d

McBride, Alex. "Brown v Board of Education." The Supreme Court. 2006. https://www.thirteen.org/wnet/supremecourt/rights/landmark_brown.html

**Chapter 3**

Henderson, William B., and Catherine Bell. "Rights of Indigenous Peoples in Canada." *The Canadian Encyclopedia*. December 11, 2019. https://bit.ly/2XWoG1b

Janken, Kenneth R. "The Civil Rights Movement: 1919–1960s." National Humanities Center. https://bit.ly/3igXvpz

Nittle, Nadra Kareem. "History of the Chicano Movement." ThoughtCo. June 22, 2020. https://bit.ly/2Prwovl

**Chapter 4**

"Commemorating the Freedom Ride." Australian Institute of Aboriginal and Torres Strait Islander Studies. February 24, 2015. https://bit.ly/3khibzz

Gentleman, Amelia. "Chased into 'self-deportation.'" *The Guardian*. September 14, 2019. https://bit.ly/39ZtqrM

**Chapter 5**

Lorenzo, Irene. "The Stonewall Uprising: 50 years of LGBT history." Stonewall. June 28, 2019. https://bit.ly/33Adg6L

Shoot, Britta. "The 1977 Disability Rights Protest That Broke Records and Changed Laws." Atlas Obscura. November 9, 2017. https://bit.ly/31obCmk

**Chapter 6**

"The Rights of Migrants in the United States." The Advocates for Human Rights. https://bit.ly/3fEo2eB

# Glossary

**Aboriginal** Relating to Indigenous people who are native to Australia

**activists** People who campaign to bring about social change

**amendments** Additions or minor changes made to a constitution

**assassinated** Murdered for political or religious reasons

**bathhouses** Houses or places in which sexual activity took place

**boycotts** Campaigns to avoid goods or services from a particular source

**caste** A traditional social class in India

**charter** A written document defining rights granted by a ruler or government

**Chicano** An American of Mexican descent

**civil disobedience** A refusal to comply with particular laws, usually as a form of peaceful political protest

**colonies** Areas governed by a country in other parts of the world

**Confederacy** The government of 11 Southern states that broke away from and fought the Union to protect their way of life, which was based on slavery

**conservative** Holds traditional views

**constitutions** Collections of basic ideas on which countries' governments are based

**deported** Removed from the country in which a person lives

**desegregated** Ended the separation of two groups, usually of different races

**discrimination** The unjust treatment of groups of people based on characteristics such as race, gender, or religion

**economic** Related to the production and distribution of goods and services

**exports** Goods sold by one country to another

**gender** The social, rather than biological, characteristics of being male or female

**guerrilla** Describes irregular warfare based on military tactics such as ambushes

**homosexuality** Being sexually attracted only to people of one's own sex

**incarcerated** Confined in prison

**Indigenous** Native to a particular place

**Middle Ages** The period of history between about 1000 and 1453

**militant** Using confrontation and violence to achieve a political goal

**nobles** Members of the elite aristocracy of a society

**non-cooperation** A refusal to cooperate with laws or authorities

**occupation** To seize a building or area by moving into it and refusing to leave

**pressure groups** Organizations that try to influence the actions of governments

**quadriplegia** Without the use of both arms and both legs

**racial profiling** Suspecting someone of a crime because of their race

**ratified** Signed, or made officially valid

**refugees** People forced to leave their countries due to war, persecution, or poverty

**round dances** Indigenous folk dances in which dancers form one large circle

**sit-ins** Protests in which activists refuse to leave a place until their demands are met

**sovereignty** The authority of a country or group to govern themselves

**status** An accepted position in a society

**systemic racism** Racism that is embedded in the laws and practices of a society or organization, rather than in the attitudes of specific individuals

**transgender** Describes a person whose gender identity is different from the sex they were assigned at birth

**unalienable** Not being able to be removed from the possessor

# Further Information

## Books


Braun, Eric. *The American Indian Rights Movement* (Movements That Matter). Minneapolis, MI: Lerner Publications, 2018.

Harris, Duchess. *LGBTQ Discrimination in America* (Being LGBTQ in America). Minneapolis, MI: Essential Library, 2019.

Honders, Christine. *Mexican American Civil Rights Movement* (Civic Participation: Working for Civil Rights). New York: PowerKids Press, 2017.

Randolph, Joanne (ed.). *African American Politicians & Civil Rights Activists* (Pioneering African Americans). New York: Enslow Publishing, 2018.

Rhuday-Perkovich, Olugbemisola. *The Civil Rights Movement* (A Step Into History). New York: Scholastic, 2018.

Thomas, Rachael L. *#BlackLivesMatter: Protesting Racism* (#movements). Minneapolis, MI: ABDO Publishing, 2019.


## Websites

**edition.cnn.com/2015/06/19/us/lgbt-rights-milestones-fast-facts/index.html**
A CNN page about the history of LGBTQ+ rights.

**www.history.com/topics/civil-rights-movement/civil-rights-movement-timeline**
An illustrated timeline of the civil rights movement from history.com.

**historyofrights.ca/history/**
An index page with links to articles about civil rights history and activism in Canada.

**hrlibrary.umn.edu/edumat/studyguides/indigenous.html**
A page from the University of Minnesota Human Rights Center that explains the rights of Indigenous peoples and why they are under threat.

**www.hrw.org/topic/disability-rights**
A Human Rights Watch page with a link to download a brochure about disability rights around the world.

**www.loc.gov/exhibits/civilrights/**
The introduction page to an extensive online exhibition about the civil rights movement from the Library of Congress.

# Index